ALL HANDS ON DECK

This book belongs to Sailor

●●●●●●●●●●●●●●●●●●●●●●●●●●●●●●

ALL HANDS ON DECK

SAILING ACTIVITY BOOK

Lisette Vos

ADLARD
COLES

LONDON · OXFORD · NEW YORK · NEW DELHI · SYDNEY

ADLARD COLES
Bloomsbury Publishing Plc
50 Bedford Square, London, WC1B 3DP, UK
29 Earlsfort Terrace, Dublin 2, Ireland

BLOOMSBURY, ADLARD COLES and the Adlard Coles logo
are trademarks of Bloomsbury Publishing Plc

First published in 2018 in the Netherlands as *Samen De Boot In*
by Hollandia BV
First published in Great Britain 2022

A catalogue record for this book is available from the British Library

ISBN: PB: 978-1-4729-8747-1
ePUB: 978-1-4729-8748-8
ePDF: 978-1-4729-8745-7

2 4 6 8 10 9 7 5 3 1

Typeset in Gotham Book by Lucy Doncaster
Printed and bound in China by Toppan Leefung Printing

FSC
www.fsc.org
MIX
Paper from
responsible sources
FSC® C104723

Contents

Sailing together, doing things together   7

1. All about boats   11

2. How boats work   19

3. Sailing rules   27

4. Find the way   35

5. On the move   43

6. Sailor on board   53

7. Fun on board   61

8. Through sunshine and storms   69

9. Sport and games   79

Are you a real sailor? Take the test!   85

Sailing diploma   89

Sailor's logbook   90

Your favourite recipe on board   93

Funny sayings   94

Draw your own flag   95

Word of thanks   96

Sailing together, doing things together

The other day, my grandson – a boy of just a year and a half – made his first trip on board my motorboat. The first thing he did was turn the steering wheel. As young as he is, he already likes to look at everything on the boat. As a proud grandfather who has sailed around the world many times on his own, I just love doing things on board with him.

All Hands on Deck lets young children discover in a playful way what sailing is all about – much more than just turning the wheel! And maybe parents or grandparents will learn something from it, too. For example, I have noticed that adults often do not realise that a boat does not always sail straight, or they don't understand why a boat with a more powerful engine can't always go faster. And I sometimes find it difficult to explain how something works on board or what it is for, as this book does so well.

When my grandson gets a little older, he'll have more questions. When this happens, he can find the answers in this book and we can have even more fun on board together! I can already see myself with a young sailor on deck who helps moor and berth, scrubs the deck, ties knots and maybe even navigates. There is no need for children on board to become bored, even if there is no Wi-Fi in the port!

Every chapter in this book is a lesson, but also an adventure. The character Sailor Taylor takes children (and their parents and grandparents!) in tow, explaining how things work in clear language. At the end of (nearly) every chapter there is then a quiz or activity. Young sailors will enjoy doing these themselves, with or without the help of the skipper.

I wish everyone on board many hours of fun with this book. Knowing how something works or what it's for is always pleasing, whether you're young or old!

Henk de Velde, round-the-world sailor

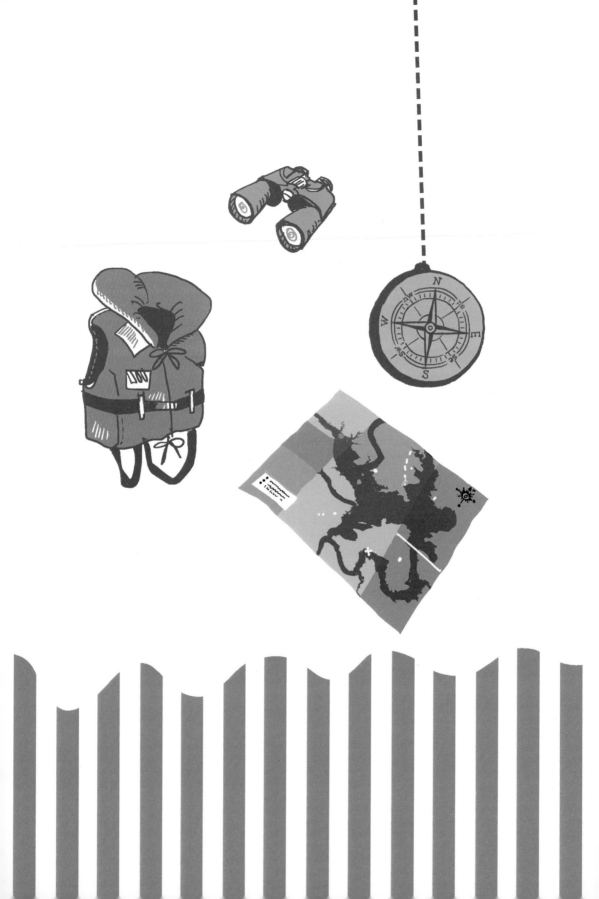

Ahoy! My name is Sailor Taylor.
On board, I like to roll up my sleeves AND have
a lot of fun. Do you also want to get started
as a sailor? In this book, you will learn all
about boats and sailing. You can also try
out activities to help you practise your new
skills. So come and jump aboard with me!

CHAPTER 1

ALL ABOUT BOATS

If you're sailing on a motorboat or a sailboat, chances are you'll see lots of different vessels along the way: big boats, small boats, fast boats, slow boats... You name it. Some boats are used to move people and goods long distances, but there are also many people who sail just for fun. Turn to pages 14–17 for more on the different types of boat.

Have you ever taken a closer look at a motorboat or sailboat? How about the boat you are sailing on or have sailed on before? Motorboats and sailboats are very different, but they are alike in many ways. Here are drawings of a motorboat and a sailboat. Shall we take a look together?

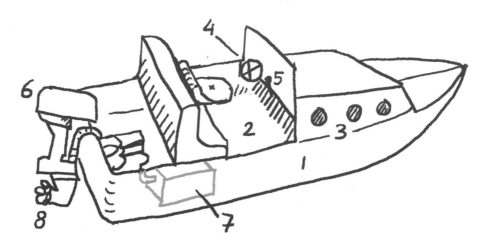

Here's what you see on a motorboat:

(1) Hull
(2) Cockpit
(3) Cabin
(4) Steering wheel/helm
(5) Throttle
(6) Engine
(7) Fuel tank
(8) Propeller

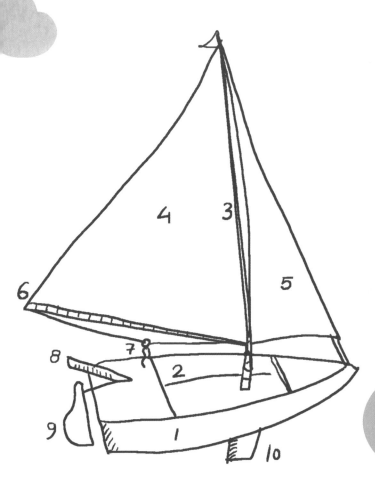

You've now taken a look at a motorboat and a sailboat. How are they different and how are they alike?

Here's what you see on a sailboat:

(1) Hull
(2) Cockpit
(3) Mast
(4) Mainsail
(5) Jib

(6) Boom
(7) Sheet
(8) Tiller
(9) Rudder
(10) Keel

Sailing for fun or for work

You now know the difference between a motorboat and a sailboat. So let's look at what types of boats and ships you might find sailing on the water. There could be quite a few of them!

There are two main types of sailing: pleasure boating and commercial shipping. In pleasure boating, the skipper and crew sail on a boat in their spare time, for fun or to relax. In commercial shipping, the skipper and crew sail on a ship for their job and to earn money. Commercial boats and ships are used to transport goods or people for a fee. But a commercial skipper and crew can also have fun on their ship.

You can sail for pleasure on these boats:

Motorboat or launch

You often see these boats on lakes and rivers. A motorboat is an open boat without a roof, so the skipper steers in the open air. There are benches on the boat so there is usually enough space for other people to sail along.

Speedboat

A speedboat has a powerful engine and glides through the water at top speeds. At full power, a speedboat goes as fast as a car! But be careful: you are not allowed to sail that fast everywhere. There are usually special areas where speedboats can go at full speed. Look out for the traffic signals!

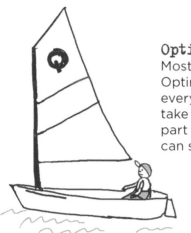

Optimist

Most young people who want to sail learn in an Optimist. This small sailing boat or dinghy has everything you need. As a young sailor, you can take sailing lessons and – if you enjoy it – take part in races organised in the Optimist class. You can spot an Optimist by the symbol on the sail.

Falcon

A Falcon is slightly bigger than an Optimist: it is a medium-sized sailing dinghy. You can sail in it for fun or – if you are a little older – race against other boats with two or three of your fellow crew members! You can also spot a Falcon by the symbol on its sail.

Rowing boat

In some boats you have to use your own strength to move forwards. For example, in a rowing boat you move the boat forwards with paddles or oars. There is no motor or wind in your sails to help you when you get tired!

You can sail for a job in these boats:

Cruise ship

On a cruise ship, passengers sail around the world, visiting different ports. A cruise ship is huge and has many floors with hundreds of rooms (and many more small windows!). That's why some people call a cruise ship a 'floating hotel'. You can do many things on board a cruise ship: shop, jump into a swimming pool or even go to the cinema.

Three-masted sailing ship

Sailing ships of the past still sail on the water, such as three-masters. The three-master gets its name from its masts. It has – you guessed it – three masts, with lots of big sails. This sailing ship used to carry goods by sea. Nowadays, you can go on a day-trip or even a short break on a three-master.

Barge

On the inland waterways, such as rivers and canals, you will see plenty of inland barges. The skipper transports goods and other items over water on this boat. Barges can carry just about anything. Nowadays, many barges are used as houseboats or people stay on them for holidays.

Ferry

Ferries carry people and goods across large bodies of water, such as lakes and rivers. A ferry always sails the same route back and forth. Before you know it, you're on the other side. Cars are allowed to ride on some ferries, but others allow only bikes. Huge ferries can carry cargo, cars and lorries across the sea.

Lifeboat

There are also boats on the water to help others, such as lifeboats. If people are in distress on a boat at sea or on a large lake, the tough men and women of the lifeboat crews come to their rescue, even when the weather is stormy.

1. Do you know your boat?

Why don't we go for a ride together on the boat you're sailing on? I wonder if you can point out all the parts you've learned? It might be fun to draw the boat and add the different parts. Ask the skipper if you need help!

2. Which boats will you see?

During a sailing trip, I always see a lot of boats. Do you want to take a look with me? What type of boats do you pass along the way? And do you know if the skipper is sailing for pleasure or doing a job? You can write down the types of boats you spot, or you can turn it into a game. I always like that! Are you in? Who can be the first person to see three barges?

3. Collecting boat names

My name is Sailor Taylor. Almost every boat also has a name. What's the name of the boat you're sailing on? Along the way, I often come across boats with funny names. Some skippers choose a cheesy name. Others choose their last name or the name of one of their children or pets. Anything is possible.

Pay attention on the way: what names have you spotted? Write them down. You'll soon have a nice collection.

4. The name game

I know another fun game with names! Say a boat name you like the sound of. Then ask the skipper or another crew member to come up with another name starting with the last letter of the name you said. And so on. For example, Taylor – Rose – Emily. Have fun!

Taylor – Rose – Emily

CHAPTER 2

HOW BOATS
WORK

Boats might look like simple machines, but they are not. It takes a lot of thought and care to build a boat. For example, a boat is designed to stay afloat, and glide through the water quickly and smoothly. Do you want to find out more? Then dive into the science and engineering of boats.

Even the skipper might learn something!

The most important thing a boat has to do is stay afloat. That may seem basic, but actually it's pretty special because not everything floats on water. If you throw a heavy brick into water, it sinks directly to the bottom. If your plastic football falls into the water, it might float away due to the wind. But it does not sink!

How is that possible? Why do some objects stay afloat and others do not?

When you put an object in the water, that object pushes away a certain amount of water. If that amount of water weighs more than the object then the object stays afloat. But if the amount of water pushed away by the object weighs less than the object, it sinks.

Water weighs almost the same as some objects:

1 litre of water is almost as heavy as a 1 kilo object.

Let's use the same plastic ball and brick from before to help us understand how this works. The ball is quite large and light (there is air inside the ball). If you push the ball underwater, it moves an amount of water that is heavier than the light ball, so the ball jumps up again and stays afloat. A brick, which is much heavier and not that big, sinks. It weighs much more than the amount of water that pushes the brick away. Maybe you have heard the saying 'sink like a stone' (or a brick)? Now you know where that comes from!

Fortunately, a boat doesn't sink like a brick. A boat is much bigger and heavier than a plastic ball, yet it still floats. This is because the amount of water a boat pushes away weighs the same or more than the boat itself. This even happens with large ships that carry a lot of heavy goods. They sit deeper in the water than empty ships and move much more water (which weighs much more). So, the skipper of a large ship doesn't have to worry about sinking!

How fast can a boat sail?

You now know why a boat stays afloat, but of course you also want to move forwards while sailing. On a motorboat, an engine is running at full power to make it speed up. A sailboat is pushed along by the wind in its sails.

But it isn't just a powerful engine or strong wind that makes some boats sail faster than others. How fast a boat goes also depends on how long the boat is. We call a boat's top speed its maximum speed. 'Maximum' means that the boat can't go any faster. When a boat can't go any faster, you will see waves around the boat: a high wave at the front *and* the back of the boat. This is also called the 'hull speed'.

LOW SPEED

HULL SPEED

If the skipper then tries to sail even harder, it usually does not work. The wave in front of the boat is so high that the boat can no longer build up extra speed. The high wave looks like a wall that the boat bumps into. No matter how much extra power the skipper uses on the motorboat, or no matter how hard the wind blows into the sails of a sailboat, it can't go faster.

Figure it out

You don't have to look at a speedometer to know how fast a boat can sail. You can do your own calculation! Use a pencil, a piece of paper and the formula below to work it out.

First of all, you need to know how long the boat is. For example, is the boat 9 metres long? Then you have to find the square root of 9 metres. It's quite complicated, so maybe you can ask the skipper for help. In this example the answer is 3, because 3 x 3 = 9. Then multiply the square root number by 4.5 to give you the maximum speed of the boat. So: 3 x 4.5 = 13.5.

So, a boat that is 9 metres long can never be faster than 13.5 kilometres per hour. That's about as fast as cycling calmly.

A longer boat can be much faster. If we use the same calculation, a boat that is 25 metres long can reach a speed of 22.5 kilometres per hour. The square root of 25 is 5, and 5 x 4.5 = 22.5.

Climbing over the wave

But beware: this calculation is not always right. Some boats can still sail faster because they can climb over the high wave in front of the boat. This is called 'planing' (or 'hydroplaning').

However, to do this, the boat must have a special shape: the back of the boat must be fairly flat. For example, a speedboat is made to sail very fast and so it has a flat back. It climbs over the high wave and skims across the surface of the water. By doing this, a speedboat can go as fast as a car on the motorway: more than 100 kilometres per hour!

PLANING OR HYDROPLANING

Gliding through the water

The people who come up with boats, the designers, make lots of different kinds of boats. There are short boats and long boats, wide boats and narrow boats, and boats that are deep or less deep in the water. The shape of the part of the boat that is underwater may also differ.

But whatever the shape or size, it is important that a motorboat or a sailboat glides easily through the water. Boats are usually a V-shape because this shape makes little contact with the water. The less the boat hits the water, the less the water slows it down. Or in other words: the smaller the resistance. If you're going boating for fun and want to go a bit faster, it helps to have less resistance!

Did you know?
When a boat sails, the movement of the boat causes waves in the water. The faster the boat sails, the higher the waves. At the front of the boat (also called the 'bow') they are called' bow waves'. At the back of the boat (also called the 'stern') they are called 'stern waves'.

ACTIVITY

1. Float or sink?

With a simple test you can discover for yourself which objects stay afloat and which sink. Fill a large bucket or container with water. Find a few objects, such as a stone, a ball, a leaf and a small plate. Guess whether the object will sink or float. Test it out. Can you explain what's happening? I'm curious!

2. How fast is your boat?

Do you want to know how fast your boat is? I do! You can do a test on board with the skipper and another crew member.

You will need: a fender (a kind of pillow that protects the boat), a long line (longer than the boat) and a stopwatch (on a watch or a smartphone).

Attach the fender to the long line. As the boat sails, the other crew member stands at the front of the boat with the fender.

You're going to stand at the back with the stopwatch. On your signal (shouting 'yes'!) the crew member throws the fender in the water at the front. That's when you press the stopwatch.

When the fender floats to the back of the boat, press the stopwatch again. You'll now know how long it took the fender to float from the front of the boat to the back. Now we can use a formula to calculate the speed in kilometres per hour. Here's how you do it.

Let's say your boat is 9 metres long, and the time on your stopwatch is, for example, 6 seconds. First, divide the length of the boat by the time, so 9 / 6 = 1.5. Next, multiply this number by 3.6. This number has been calculated to give the right answer. Do this calculation and you'll know the speed.

So, in this example: 1.5 x 3.6 = 5.4 kilometres per hour. You can use this calculation for all boats, whether they are short or long!

3. What is the best shape for a boat?

What shape does a boat need to be to glide through the water easily? You can find out with this little test!

You will need: a stick about 0.5 metres long, three ropes or lines (one long line of about 3 or 4 metres and two shorter lines of about 1.5 metres), and two objects that you can drag through the water – for example, a milk carton and a soda bottle.

Tie the long line to the middle of the stick. Next, tie the objects (one at either end) to the stick using the shorter lines of equal length. Hold onto the end of the long line and throw the stick, with objects attached, into the water behind the boat and let the objects drag through the water. Make sure the stick doesn't touch the water. More importantly, don't allow the line to get stuck in the propeller!

Watch the objects closely to see which is slowed down the most by the water (or, in other words, has the most resistance). You'll know because the stick attached to that object will be pulled backwards. That object has the shape that glides less well through the water.

You can do this test as many times as you like, to find out what shape a boat should have so that it glides through the water most easily. For example, you can also make your own boats out of polystyrene or plastic containers of different shapes and lengths, and which lie deeper or less deep in the water. Make sure that you take your containers home with you when you've finished the experiment.

CHAPTER 3

SAILING
RULES

House rules, school rules, spelling rules... how many rules are there? I'm sure you don't always like following them, but they usually exist for a reason. It's no different on the water. If each skipper follows the sailing rules, it is more fun and safer for everyone.

If you want to go boating, it's very likely that you won't be the only one on the water. While out and about, you can run into all types of vessels, from small to large: canoes, rowing boats, sailboats, speedboats, tour boats, barges, cargo ships – you name it! This makes it extra fun on the water, but all these vessels cannot criss-cross through one another's path.

Unlike on roads, there are no lines to tell you where everyone is allowed to sail. And on the water, there are no traffic lights that tell you whether or not you can continue on your journey. How are you supposed to know when and where to go and when to stop? Fortunately, there are sailing rules that every skipper must follow.

Priority rules: who goes first? − − − − − − − − −

On the water there are priority rules, just like on land. If you're in a car at a roundabout, you usually have to check and wait for any cars coming from the right in the United Kingdom (the direction changes according to what country you are driving in). They have priority.

Starboard has priority
When two motorboats of the same size approach each other, the right one has priority over the left one. But skippers don't talk about right and left – they say 'starboard' and 'port'.

How do you remember which is which? Here's an easy way. 'Star' from starboard rhymes with 'r'. 'R' is the first letter in 'right', so starboard is right. Port and left have four letters each, so port is left.

Look at the sails!
The rule is different when two sailboats approach each other. In that case, you need to look at the sails. A sailboat with the sail on the port side (the left side) has priority over a sailboat with the sail on the starboard side (on the right).

Large boats have priority

There are times when the priority rules do not apply. For example, a large cargo ship, often longer than 20 metres, has priority over smaller boats. This is also the case if the smaller boat comes from the right (starboard). There is a reason for this. Large cargo ships are harder to turn or slow down than smaller motorboats or sailboats. So, the smaller boats have to swerve to give priority to a large cargo ship.

And that's not all: a small motorboat can make a turn faster or slow down faster than a small sailboat. This means – you guessed it – that a small sailboat has priority over a small motorboat.

Good seamanship

If everyone follows the rules, everything should be OK, don't you think? Unfortunately, that's not always the case. Because a boat does not have brakes, unlike a bicycle or a car, a skipper cannot stop quite as easily. So sometimes it's smarter to give priority to another boat, although the rules say otherwise.

We call this 'good seamanship'. This rule means you have to be thoughtful and act safely in any situation. After all, it is your job as a skipper to make sure that two boats do not collide. No one wants that, right?

— Flags on board ——————————————

If you pay attention, you'll see different flags on a lot of boats, in all kinds of sizes, shapes and colours. Not only does it look very festive, but the flags also have meanings.

National flag

You probably know your own country's flag and what colours are on it. On a motorboat or sailboat, the national flag is the most important flag: everyone on the water can see which country the boat comes from. The boat's national flag always flies on a flagpole on the back of the ship, but only during the day when the skipper is on board or sailing!

Courtesy flag

If you sail abroad or in a different region of your country, you can raise the courtesy flag. For example, if you are sailing in France, you will fly the French flag. It's a way to greet everyone in the country or region where you are a guest. Which is very polite, isn't it? This flag is small in size and hangs on the right (starboard) side of the mast.

Did you know?

You might think a flagship is just a ship with flags. That's right, but it also means something else. The skipper of a flagship is in charge of a number of ships sailing together, called a 'fleet'. That skipper has a special name: the 'admiral'!

NED
12

31

Owner's flag

This is the flag of the owner of the boat. It can be the owner's flag or a visitor's flag – the skipper can choose. For example, this flag may show something related to the boat's name. You raise the owner's flag on the mast. It sits under the courtesy flag.

Signal flags

Then there are the signal flags. These provide important information, especially about the large ships sailing at sea. In total, there are 40 flags that give important information about a boat.

If a person has fallen overboard on a ship, a skipper must do everything they can to seek help fast. To do this, they can raise the 'Man overboard' flag on the mast: a rectangular flag with a yellow and red triangle. Anyone who is in the area with a ship will know what is going on and hopefully come to the rescue!

Flag line

You can also decorate the boat with dozens of colourful flags when there is a party to celebrate, for example if it is your birthday or just because it is the first day of the holidays. If you attach flags to a special long flag line, the boat will soon look festive. On this line, you can also hang pennants, which are small, colourful flags in the shape of a pointed triangle.

It's likely that you'll run into a lot of boats on the water along the way. These can be small or large, with a sail or with a motor. Some skippers sail for pleasure, others are at work and carry cargo on their ship. When everyone on a boat – you too! – knows the sailing rules, it becomes more fun and safer for everyone on the water.

Check out the three drawings on the right – I've drawn boats and ships of all shapes and sizes on the water. Take a good look.

Now test your knowledge of the rules on the water with this quick quiz. Do you know the right answers?

Question 1:
Which motorboat (a or b) has priority?

Question 2:
Do you see cargo ship c and sailboat d? Who is approaching from starboard?

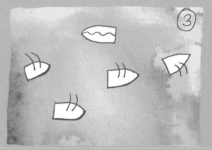

Question 3:
How many sailboats with the sail on port side do you see?

If you want to practise some more, ask the skipper to come up with some questions for you!

Question 1: Motorboat b. Question 2: Sailing boat d. Question 3: 3 sailboats.

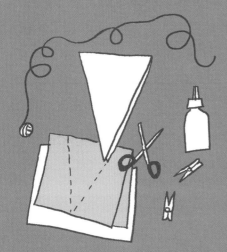

Design your own flag or flag line

I always feel happy when I see flags on a boat. Do you? As we just discussed, if you want to raise a flag on the mast, you have to follow the rules. But you can also make your own flags and pennants.

What kind of flag would you like to draw – perhaps a tough pirate flag or maybe a colourful pennant with a picture of your boat on it? (There is space for you to draw your flag on page 95 in this book.)

You can make a flag line on the boat by creating multiple pennants. Get a long line (rope or ribbon) and hang lots of paper or fabric pennants on it. Here's how.

You will need:
- scissors
- a piece of thick cardboard
- patches of fabric or paper shapes
- a clothes peg
- a long line (rope or ribbon)
- glue or textile glue

First, cut the shape of a pennant out of the cardboard, to use as your template.

Now fold a piece of fabric or a sheet of paper in half, place the cardboard pennant between the folds and attach it with a clothes peg. Cut the folded paper or the fabric, using the cardboard pennant as a guide.

You can then hang the paper or fabric pennant over the line and glue the two sides together to fix it in place. If you use fabric, you will need special textile glue.

Repeat the process to make more pennants to hang on your line, and decorate them as you like.

CHAPTER 4

FIND THE WAY

Fancy a boat trip? Just start the engine or hoist the sails! But how do you find your way on the water? To start with, you can simply take a good look around you to see what you can see. It is also important to keep a water map on board (also called a 'chart' in sailing terms). This will show you the way, exactly like a map on land. Can you lend a helping hand to the skipper?

There's nothing more fun than being on a boat trip, snuggled up on deck, with the wind in your hair. Don't you think? You can go in all directions on the water. Do you want to sail to a quiet island or to a port where there is lots to do and see?

On rivers, canals, lakes and the sea you can sail thousands of kilometres. But road signs that show the way, such as those found on land, do not exist on the water. This means that it can be quite tricky to find the right route.

Look around

Luckily, you don't have to get lost on the water. If you look around you, there are lots of clues to help you see where you are. In the past, skippers looked for lighthouses and tall church towers on land near the sea or a village to help them work out where they were. They still do this today. So, you can help the skipper by being the lookout.

And have you noticed the green and red buoys and markers on the water? They are there for a reason: they tell us which way the boat is sailing. If the red markers and buoys are on the right side of the water and the green ones on the left, you are sailing away from land and out to sea.

If you sail from the sea towards land, it is the other way around: the buoys and markers on the left side are red and on the right side they are green.

And, oh yes, here's another fact: when it's dark, only the buoys along the water can help you find your way around. There is a large light on a buoy, not on a marker. That's the difference between a buoy and a marker.

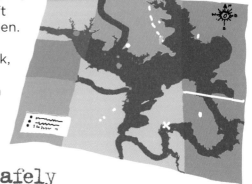

Charts: finding your way safely

So, looking around helps you to figure out where you are on the water. But with a water map (or chart) on board, you'll be better prepared. Just as there are road maps for driving on land, there are water maps with blue waterways for boats.

For centuries, skippers have used paper water maps to sail around the world. Nowadays, it's just as easy to map out the route on a smartphone or tablet screen. A paper map does have one big advantage, though: you can be sure the battery will never run out!

There is so much to discover on a water map. All waterways – water you can sail on, such as rivers, canals, lakes and the sea – are coloured blue on a map. If you look closely, you'll see the red and green buoys and markers that show you the way when you're sailing out to sea or heading towards land. On the blue waterways, you'll also see the bridges and locks that you will come across along the way. If you want to discover even more, look at the legend in the corner of the map. This tells you what all the different colours and symbols on the map mean.

A water map not only helps the skipper to find the route, but also to sail safely to another place or port. That's kind of useful to know, don't you think? For example, you can see on the map where the water is shallow or how high a bridge is. This is useful, since it means the boat won't get stuck on the bottom or you'll know to avoid a low bridge if your boat has a tall mast.

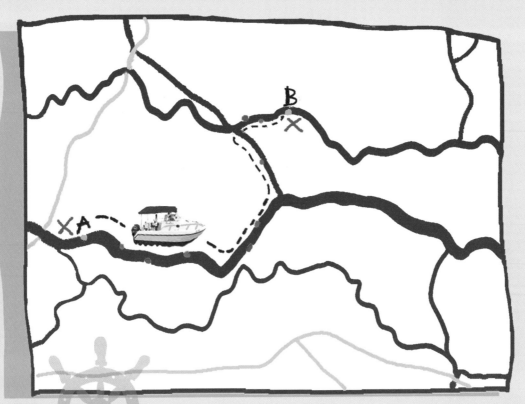

Sailing on a compass

But there's even more on the water map. Do you see the compass rose, which shows the directions north, east, south and west? As a sailor, you can bring your own compass on board. It shows you the direction in which you are sailing.

The compass needle always points north (to the top of the water map), whatever direction you're turning the compass in. Try it!

How is this possible? It's quite complicated, but let me try to explain. The Earth is one big magnet and the red needle of the compass is magnetic. These two magnets – the northernmost part of the Earth and the red compass needle – attract each other. That's why the red needle always points north.

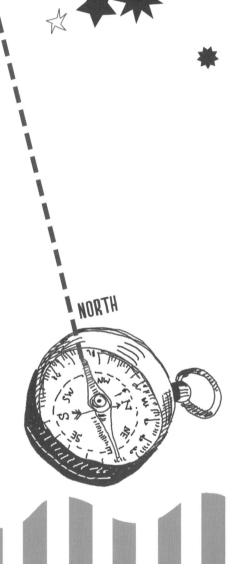

NORTH

Dot on a screen

Nowadays, the skipper has to do less and less to find his way. This is because many boats have a device on board on which they can follow the route of the boat on a screen while sailing along – just like the satellite navigation in a car. A moving dot on the screen then shows where you are sailing. Handy, isn't it?

Did you know?
Stars in the sky also show you the way. In the past, skippers and sailors knew which way to go by keeping an eye on the Pole Star at night. If they could find that special star among all the other stars in the sky, they could find where north was. During the day, the position of the sun was helpful. Every day, the sun rises in the east and sets in the west.

Map out a sailing route

Now you know there are many ways to find your way on the water. Remember to take a water map (chart) with you. And don't forget your compass, which can help you find your way. Practice drawing a route on the water map below.

Where are we going?

ACTIVITY

Is the route ready? Then let's sail!

Do you have a plan for a boat trip? If so, then with the skipper's help, we can map out the sailing route. A paper map will come in handy. It shows a much bigger area than you can see on the small screen of a smartphone or a tablet. If you know where you want to go, mark two places on the water map: the place where the boat is now, and where you want to sail to.

Together with the skipper, you can map out the route on the water map. In which direction will you sail: north, east, south or west? What will you come across on the water along the way? Will you see red and green buoys or markers? How many bridges and locks can you count on the route? What port are you going to arrive at?

I know from experience that you can go in many directions on the water. I find it helpful to draw the route before I go sailing, so that I know what to expect. See the example on page 38.

Is the route ready? Then let's sail!
You can help the skipper by looking around you while sailing. What do you see? I also have another tip for you! Use the water map you have drawn and the compass to check you are heading in the right direction.

Follow the dot on the screen
Sometimes I'm a bit lazy! You too? If the boat has an electronic device with a map on board or if the skipper has a smartphone or a tablet with a chart or map, then you don't have to try quite as hard. You can simply follow the moving dot on the screen along the way. The dot shows you where to sail! Just to be safe, though, keep the paper map and compass close by. If your smartphone or tablet runs out of battery or breaks, you still want to be able to find your way!

CHAPTER 5

ON THE MOVE

Do you have your route mapped out? On a water map you can see much more than just the sea. Look for harbours or places where you can moor your boat. Lighthouses mark cliffs and dangerous rocks. But that's not all: the map also shows the depth of the water, and you may even see where there is a shipwreck under the sea.

On rivers and canals, if you look closely at the water map, you'll spot bridges and locks you'll meet along the way. That's useful to know. You must be able to sail under the bridge (if it cannot open). And if you have to sail through a lock, it takes extra time. Are you well prepared?

Bridges and locks come in all shapes and sizes. Some are big enough for huge ships to sail under or through them. Whatever their size, it's likely that you'll come across one at some point.

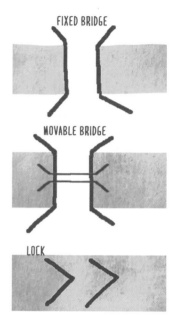

FIXED BRIDGE

MOVABLE BRIDGE

LOCK

A lock: a lift in the water

When you travel on rivers and canals, you can't always just continue, because the water is not at the same level everywhere. Fortunately, locks can take boats from one water height to another (higher or lower). So, a lock is a bit like a lift. But how exactly does it work?

If you meet a lock along the way, the first thing you'll notice are big gates in the water. In a big lock, the lock keeper gives the signal that you can enter the lock. In smaller locks on canals, you might need to open the gates yourself. Once you are in the lock, the gates close again, and the water slowly goes up or down.

This is how it works: on the other side of the lock, a valve opens underwater, so that water either runs into or out of the lock. When the water inside the lock reaches the same height as the water outside the lock, the gates open again. When the lock keeper gives the signal, or if the lights are green, you can leave the lock.

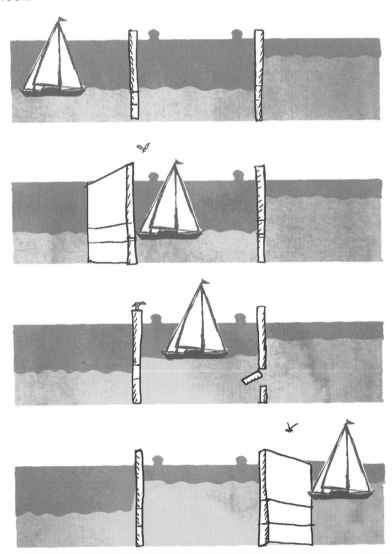

Rules in a lock

If you want or need to sail through a lock, you have to be patient and follow the rules. First of all, there must be a space for the boat in the lock. In summer, some locks can get crowded, and you can end up in a real boat traffic jam!

Once you have made it to the front of the queue, you'll have to wait some time to go through the lock. This is because it takes a while for the gates to open, close and reopen.

To make sure everything runs smoothly, there are a few rules to follow. They're not very strict, but if all skippers stick to them, it's more fun and safer for everyone on the water.

Is it crowded in front of the lock? Then wait your turn. If a commercial boat wants to sail into the lock, it has priority over pleasure boats. The skipper on your motorboat or sailboat must give the boat priority.

In the lock, the skipper needs to moor the boat to the wall. So, together with the skipper, find a good spot and get the lines and the fenders (which protect the boat from the lock wall and from other boats) ready. Attach the boat to the lock wall by laying lines around the bollards (a kind of pole) in the wall.

Don't pull the lines too tight! The water goes up or down, and you don't want the boat to be tilted by a tight line. Make sure that the lines can move with the water going up or down.

Mooring your boat

If you're not sailing through a lock, you can still help the skipper and be a useful crew member. When the boat is coming into harbour, you can hang out the fenders and prepare the mooring ropes. This means the boat can moor up smoothly without any bumps and scrapes. When you're ready to leave the mooring, the skipper will need help to untie the mooring lines and make sure everything is tidy.

Always keep a lookout for other boats and shout to the skipper if you see a boat moving on the port or starboard side.

Did you know?

The sea lock at Ijmuiden, in the Netherlands, is no less than 500 metres long, 70 metres wide and 18 metres deep. It's the biggest lock in the world! The sea lock was built almost a hundred years ago and it has been made bigger, because the seagoing vessels that want to enter the Netherlands are now much larger than they were before. For motorboats and sailboats that want to sail at sea, there is a smaller lock located next to the big one.

As you sail around, you'll usually come across a few bridges. These carry road traffic from one side of the water to the other. When you're in a boat, you can't get around a bridge, you have to go under it. You may think that a bridge is a bridge, but there are many different types, built in a special way. Some may open – called movable bridges; others don't – called fixed bridges.

Drawbridge
The road surface of a drawbridge can be lifted up completely or in two parts. If a boat is too high to go under the bridge when it is in its normal position, the bridge must be raised. Tower Bridge on the River Thames in London is a famous drawbridge.

Lift bridge
When a lift bridge opens, the road surface is raised up and it stays horizontal. In Rotterdam in the Netherlands there is a lift bridge that has the nickname 'De Hef' ('the Lift'). There used to be trains running over this bridge.

Cable-stayed bridge
On this type of bridge, the road surface hangs directly from high poles by steel cables. There are examples of cable-stayed bridges all over the world. They must be high enough for boats to sail underneath.

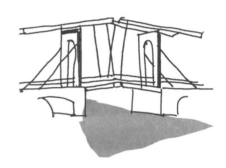

Arch bridge
An arch bridge is recognisable by the fact that there is an arch or several arches on the bridge. One example is the famous Sydney Harbour Bridge in Australia.

Signs and lights on bridges

If you're sailing near a bridge, pay close attention to any signs or symbols on it, like the ones on the right. They sometimes also have lights. If you see any of these, make sure you find out what they mean. They tell you important information, such as whether you can continue sailing and which way you need to go through the bridge.

There are some movable bridges, especially on canals, that you need to open yourself, with the help of other members of your crew. Signs will tell you if this is the case. Some movable bridges also have lights. If you only see red lights, it means that you can't sail under the bridge.

Some big movable bridges can only be opened if a bridge keeper operates the bridge. In this case, of course you need to know when this is going to happen so that you can time it right and pass through. If you see a green light appear under the red lights – on the left- and right-hand sides of the bridge – this is a signal that you'll soon be able to sail on.

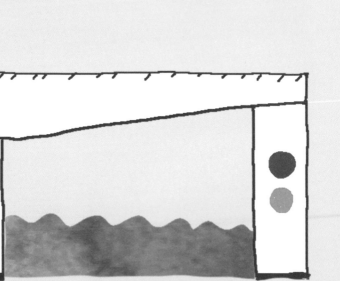

As well as bridges, you may see buildings by the water. At the coast, you may spot tall lighthouses to warn sailors about dangers. At night, you can see the beams of light from the lighthouse flashing or zooming around the sky. You may also come across tall harbour walls and structures such as cranes for lifting boats in and out of the water or unloading cargo ships.

On rivers and canals, you may see a special cottage for the keeper who opens a movable bridge or a lock. Many of these cottages are no longer in use because boaters work the locks themselves.

In the past, in the Netherlands, a bridge keeper would often throw out a fishing rod from the bridge with a small clog attached. This was so that the skippers could put bridge money or a tip in it to thank the keeper for opening the bridge.

Look out! ▬ ▬ ▬ ▬ ▬ ▬ ▬ ▬ ▬ ▬ ▬ ▬

Sailing boats that have tall masts can only pass under very tall bridges. Boats for sailing inland are often quite low and narrow so they can easily go through lower bridges and locks.

Sailing boats often have a keel (a fin on the bottom of the boat), too. This means the skipper has to be careful that the water is not too shallow. Skippers need to use a water map or electronic device to check that the water is deep enough so that the keel does not get stuck.

When you sail at sea, you need to think about the weather and which direction the wind is blowing as you make your journey.

Wherever you sail, there are always lots of things you need to think about and plan for.

Logbook: a journal on the water

Are you going to take a long boat trip of one or more days? Then it's fun to keep a logbook. This is a kind of diary in which you write down everything about your sailing experience and what you encounter along the way. Every day, you can write down the sailing information – everything from the route you take to the weather forecast, and from the bridges and locks you come across to the port where you dock.

And of course, you should write down the name of the boat, of the skipper and yours as a sailor – and of the other sailors.

There is space on page 90 to create a log. Alternatively, you can also buy a new notebook to use as your log!

A journal on the water

CHAPTER 5
SAILOR ON BOARD

We're going aboard. Are you ready, sailor? Ahoy! On the boat, you're the skipper's helper. You are on the lookout, can assist with mooring at the pier or make the boat shiny again. The skipper could use your help. All hands on deck!

If you're going to sail, of course you can laze around on the deck. But isn't it much more fun to help the skipper? Put on your sailor's cap and get to work.

As a sailor, you have important tasks on board. In the past, sailors on large sailing ships that sailed by sea had to work hard and listen to the captain, who was in charge of the ship. They had to keep watch and be on the lookout, hoist the sails, tie knots and, last but not least, scrub the deck to keep the ship clean. They didn't have much free time, although sometimes they could laze around in a hammock or play music together. But not for too long!

Before you leave port, think about what you need on board so that you can help the skipper. If you are the lookout, it is useful to have a pair of binoculars. If you want to keep an eye on whether the skipper is sailing in the right direction, don't forget your compass (see page 39). And bring some extra ropes (on the boat these are called 'lines') to make knots, for example to moor the boat in the harbour.

Lastly, if you want to be a real sailor then you're going to need a bucket and a deck mop to scrub the deck. Then you can help to keep things clean!

Are you ready to roll up your sleeves?

Roll up your sleeves!

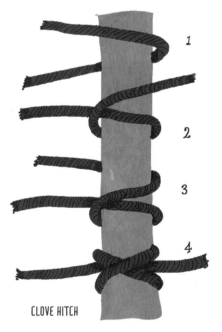

Did you know?
A knot is a tie in a rope or line, but it also means something else. It tells you the speed of a ship. 1 knot = 1 nautical mile per hour. Do you want to know how many kilometres per hour a knot is? It's almost 2 kilometres per hour, or 1.852 to be precise.

As a sailor, of course, you don't want the lines on the boat to get tangled. If you know how to tie knots, it saves a lot of time. A correct knot is tight and – very importantly – can be untied quickly and easily.

You can use knots and hitches for different purposes: to tie lines together, to attach a line to something else (for example, to a boat mast) or to make a loop (which you can throw around a pole or bollard in the harbour).

Why don't we learn how to tie a few knots together? Take a good look at the pictures below. If at first you don't succeed in tying a knot, listen to the skipper. Tying knots takes practice!

With a clove hitch you can attach a line to a mast on a boat or a pole, for example. With a bowline you can make a loop with which you can moor the boat on to a bollard. You can use a reef knot to tie two lines together.

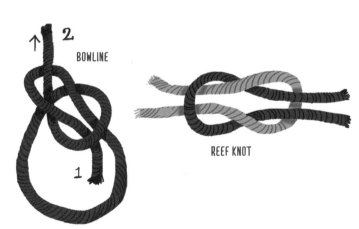

1

2

3

4

CLOVE HITCH

2

↑ BOWLINE

1

REEF KNOT

— Docking in the harbour ━ ━ ━ ━ ━ ━ ━ ━ ━ ━ ━ ━

Sailing a boat is very different to driving a vehicle on the road. 'Parking' – mooring a boat in the harbour or at the quayside – can be quite difficult. Even an experienced skipper sometimes needs help to moor.

Unlike on the road, the conditions on the water are always different. The water moves, with a weak or a strong current. The wind also affects mooring a boat on the quay. Sometimes the wind blows from the land towards the water – we call this 'windward shore' – and sometimes the wind blows towards the land – we call this 'leeward shore'. The wind direction can make a bit of a difference for the docking, but a good skipper knows how to handle it!

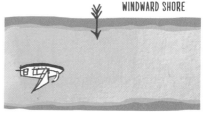

WINDWARD SHORE

LEEWARD SHORE

A sailor helps to moor by attaching the lines to the bollards on the land (on the quay or on the pier). That can be a hard job! You can also hang the fenders outboard, to prevent the boat from bumping or scraping if the skipper accidentally sails against the quay. Have the lines ready on board so that you or an adult sailor can put a loop around a bollard in one move. This doesn't always work the first time. You can practise when the boat is moored at the quayside. Take the lines in your hands, have a good look and just throw.

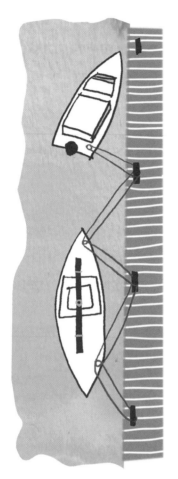

Another fun fact: the lines used to fasten a boat are called 'mooring lines'. Usually, you need four lines to attach the boat to a bollard on land. Lines that you fasten in front of or behind the boat on the land are called 'bow lines' or 'stern lines'. You can also attach the lines to land from the side of the boat. Then they're called 'springs'. So go ahead and throw the lines and springs! But be careful not to fall into the water between the shore and the ship...

Anchoring

Does the boat have an anchor on board? If the answer is yes, then you can lie at anchor! This is where you can find a nice spot in the middle of the water and lower the anchor quietly. Once the anchor has landed at the bottom, the boat remains in one place. Now you can enjoy yourself!

An anchor is also useful if the boat has engine trouble or if the rudder stops working. You can use it to make sure the boat doesn't drift off. This can prevent accidents, especially in a busy sailing area.

Safety on board

One more thing! Safety is the most important thing on board, for all sailors. You don't want to fall overboard. So, listen carefully to the skipper and always pay attention. Even if you can swim, you should always wear a lifejacket while sailing on a boat. Just do it!

1. Create a knot board

I've made a lot of knots in my life. Now it's your turn! On page 56 there are three examples of knots that you can practise. But there are many more knots and hitches (search online for how to tie different ones). Other types of knot are the sheet bend, the figure eight knot and the half hitch.

It's simple to make a knot board using all these knots and hitches. How? You will need a board (of thick cardboard or soft board), rope (not too thick), tape or thumbtacks, scissors, and paper on which you can write the names of the various knots and hitches.

When you've finished your knot board, hang it in a special place on board the boat!

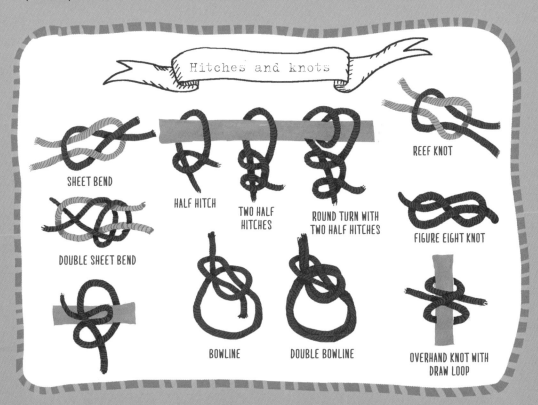

Hitches and knots

SHEET BEND

HALF HITCH

TWO HALF HITCHES

ROUND TURN WITH TWO HALF HITCHES

REEF KNOT

DOUBLE SHEET BEND

FIGURE EIGHT KNOT

BOWLINE

DOUBLE BOWLINE

OVERHAND KNOT WITH DRAW LOOP

2. Knots made of liquorice laces and spaghetti

You can tie knots with a piece of rope, but you can also do it in another way. With liquorice laces it's even more fun!

You can also turn it into a game to play with the other sailors (or the skipper). Who can turn two liquorice laces into a flat knot the fastest? The winner gets to eat the liquorice laces!

Practising with cooked strands of spaghetti does the job just as well. And then you can eat the rest of the spaghetti while on board. Enjoy your meal!

CHAPTER 7

FUN ON
BOARD

You might think you have nothing to do during a boat trip, but as a sailor there is always plenty on a boat to keep you entertained. This is also true on a rainy day in the harbour – you should never get bored! Try building a boat or singing sea shanties, or cooking a skipper's meal and writing a message in a bottle. Are you in?

Building a small boat

Boats are not made in a factory. Instead, they are built in a boatyard, or a shipyard for bigger ships. There, the shipbuilders put the parts of the boat together. Boats are built from different materials such as steel, plastic or wood. When the work is done, the builders launch the boat in the water. Large ships slide into the water from a sloping slipway. Often, that's an occasion to have a party! It's traditional for shipbuilders to smash a bottle of champagne against the new ship. They wish the ship and the crew a safe journey!

Do you know what material the boat you're sailing on is made of? If you want to make your own boat, you can also make it from different materials. You can start with paper.

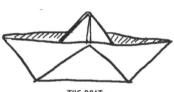

THE BOAT

A small boat made of paper

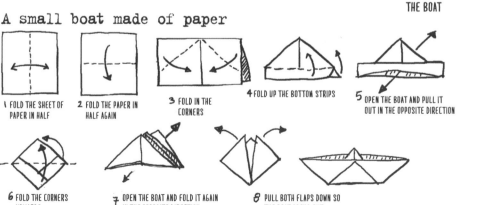

1 FOLD THE SHEET OF PAPER IN HALF

2 FOLD THE PAPER IN HALF AGAIN

3 FOLD IN THE CORNERS

4 FOLD UP THE BOTTOM STRIPS

5 OPEN THE BOAT AND PULL IT OUT IN THE OPPOSITE DIRECTION

6 FOLD THE CORNERS UPWARDS

7 OPEN THE BOAT AND FOLD IT AGAIN IN THE OPPOSITE DIRECTION

8 PULL BOTH FLAPS DOWN SO THE BOAT OPENS OUT

A raft made of wooden lollipop sticks

You will need about 30 wooden lollipop sticks. Place 9 sticks side by side. Place another layer of 9 sticks on top, but give them a quarter turn. Glue them down. For the third layer, add 9 more sticks in the same direction as the bottom layer. Make a small hole in the middle stick, in which you can fix the stick mast with glue. Attach a small paper sail to the mast (with two small cuts in the sail, through which the mast can pass). Let's sail!

A raft made of branches

If you are near a forest or are on an island with lots of trees, you can collect branches to build a raft. Collect branches that have fallen to the ground: never cut them off a tree that is living. The branches should all be roughly the same thickness and length. Place the branches side by side and tie them together with rope. This is your raft. Place two more branches ('sleepers') across the raft and fasten well. Now put the raft in the water. Does it stay afloat? Good job!

A large motorboat made from a milk carton

A cardboard milk carton is almost a kind of boat in itself – it is designed to keep liquid inside rather than outside. Cut the carton in half lengthways to make the tub (ask an adult to help you). On both sides, cut two round shapes out of the carton to make the windows in the boat. These round windows are also called 'portholes'. You can decorate the boat as much as you like. Don't forget the flag!

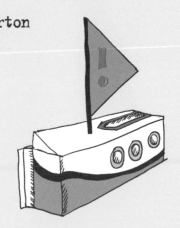

Are you excited to be a sailor? It's just as fun to read stories about brave sea heroes of the past. You can read about explorers who sailed to places that were unknown in Europe, such as Captain James Cook, who visited Australia, New Zealand and many places in the Pacific Ocean.

We like to read stories of pirates and daring adventurers on the oceans. Sailing ships carried big cannons that fired cannon balls at enemies.

There are also modern sea heroes, who sail around the world on small boats and overcome storms and other dangers.

Did you know?
When you're by the sea, you might spot a boatyard where boats are built and repaired. When you see a boat out of the water, it can seem much bigger than it does when most of the boat and the keel is underwater.

Older boats are made of wood and the sailing ships of the past were wooden. Modern boats are made of other materials, such as fibreglass or steel.

Sailor

Tattoos

Tough sailors often have tattoos on their upper arms. They usually choose pictures that have something to do with sailing at sea. A boat, an anchor or a mermaid – anything is possible! Or sometimes they get a big heart with their sweetheart's name underneath.

Real ink tattoos cannot be removed. But it can be fun to play with temporary stickers. They remain on your arm for a while and are easy to wash off. Just as tough!

Sailor becomes ship's cook

If you're on board for a long time and are working hard all day, make sure you eat well. On large ships, there is a ship's cook who prepares food for everyone on board. The recipes are usually simple and filling. It is especially important that the meal is nutritious. This means that the cook often has to peel a lot of potatoes!

It's not easy cooking a meal while on board a boat. The kitchen, or 'galley', can be very cramped and the boat may be moving around in a rough sea. For this reason, it's best to keep the meals simple for the skipper and crew.

Do you have a favourite skipper's meal that you like to prepare on the boat? There is space to write it down at the end of the book (see page 93).

Message in a bottle

In the past, there were no smartphones, so you couldn't make video calls or send a text to your friends. If you wanted to send a message, all you could do was write a letter and post it by mail. Of course, you can still do that!

Write a letter (and why not add a nice drawing), which includes the date and where the skipper can be reached. Ask the finder if they want to respond. Next, put the letter inside a glass bottle that you can seal really well, and close it. If you make the bottle a little heavier (for example with sand), it is more likely to travel further.

Choose a day when the wind is blowing away from the land and throw your bottle into the sea or some flowing water. Otherwise, the message won't get very far!

It's now a question of wait and see. You don't know who's going to get the message in a bottle. That just makes it extra exciting.

You don't always have to throw your message in a bottle in the water. If you want to ask your friends to come to your birthday party, you can hand out your invitation as a message in a bottle. This way, you'll be sure your mail will arrive!

Sea shanties (sailor's songs)

When sailors on board sing loudly, everybody has a good time. Sea shanties are songs that sailors sing as they work, setting the sails or pulling up the anchor.

You'll find lots of sea shanties on the internet (YouTube is a good place to start). Find the lyrics and sing along. Are you in? You can sing as loud as you want! Here's an example:

Away, haul away, we'll haul away Joe
(To me) way, haul away
We'll heave and hang together
Away, haul away, we'll haul away Joe

Did you know that there are many sayings about boats and sailing? For instance, we might say someone is left 'high and dry', which means they can't go anywhere (like a boat when it's out of the water). If someone is in trouble we could say they are 'sailing close to the wind'. Another example of a saying? When we're very busy, we say we need 'all hands on deck', which means everyone on board needs to help.

Would you like to know more about sayings? Go to a search engine online and type in 'sayings' and keywords such as 'boat', 'ship' and 'sail'. I'm sure you'll come across some fun examples.

At the end of this book there is space to write down some of your favourite sayings about boats and sailing (see page 94).

CHAPTER 8

THROUGH SUNSHINE AND STORMS

Whether you're sailing on a motorboat or a sailboat, it's always smart to check the weather forecast before you set off. On a boat, you don't want to get caught in a violent storm. When you're sailing, you are even more dependent on the weather. To speed up, the sail must catch enough wind. But how do you know you can count on the weather?

What is your ideal sailing weather? Do you like lazing in the sun on deck? Or do you find sailing in high winds and big waves exciting? The weather can change fast and every day is different. For example, there can be a storm in the spring or summer, not just in autumn or winter.

Fortunately, there are experts who know how to predict what the weather is going to be. They're called 'meteorologists'.

How do you predict the weather?

You can find weather forecasts on television, on the radio and on the internet. Weathercasters forecast and report the weather on television. They use weather maps to tell us whether we can expect rain, clouds or a sunny day. You can also look up the weather on the internet. This will tell you if there will be showers in the coming hours and where it will rain. You can also find out how strong the wind will be. Pretty handy!

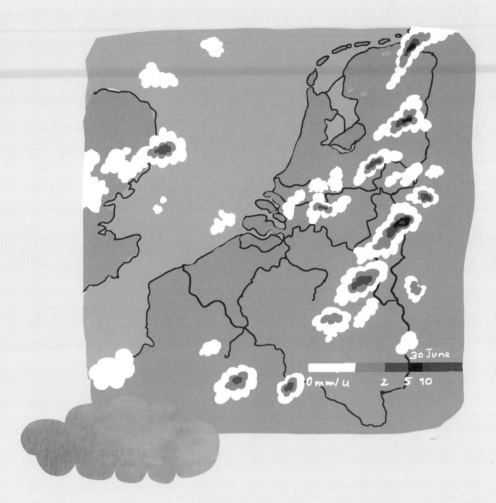

30 June

0 mm/u   2   5 10

Behind the scenes, experts are working on the weather forecast. They use computers that collect all kinds of data. For example, they take lots of measurements in many places, including air pressure, wind direction and temperature. This helps to create a weather forecast. But remember: this is a prediction. Weathercasters can never be 100 per cent sure what the weather is going to be like, although they often get it right!

Can you predict the weather yourself?

You can't change the weather, but you can plan around it. But where do you begin? Simple - take a look outside!

Watching the clouds

Clouds in the sky can help you to better predict the weather. A cloud is made up of countless water droplets. With a little bad luck, it will turn into a rainstorm.

When you look up at the clouds, you'll learn a lot about the weather. If there are no clouds in the sky and the sky is clear and blue, it's probably going to be a sunny day. If you see big dark clouds in the distance, be warned: bad weather with rain is coming your way! You don't need a weathercaster to tell you that.

Small paintings in the sky

We can learn a lot about the weather by looking at the clouds. But have you ever noticed that clouds are different shapes? Maybe you've seen sheep clouds in the sky before? They look - you guessed it - like sheep. Clouds appear in so many different forms, and they often change shape so quickly that some people can look at them for hours. Sometimes they're like paintings in the sky.

Clouds high and low

There are many different types of clouds. There is low, medium and high cloud cover. Some clouds hang just above the ground and other clouds are more than 10 kilometres up in the sky. Different types of clouds have their own names.

When the clouds are just above the ground, we call it fog. Then you literally walk or sail with your head through the clouds and sometimes you can no longer see your hand in front of your face.
For a skipper on a boat, that's no fun! You might hear a fog horn across the water to warn you that another boat is nearby, even if you can't see it.

Foggy day? Lights on!

When there is poor visibility during the day, skippers should turn on the lights on the boat. This helps other skippers on the water to see the boat through the fog, and you to see where you're going! As you know, boats have a white light in the mast and/or at the back, red lights on the left of the boat (port) and green lights on the right of the boat (starboard). These lights are called 'navigation lights', because they show the way. If a boat has no lights, you can't sail if it is foggy or dark.

The wind blows ▬ ▬ ▬ ▬ ▬ ▬

You can't sail without the wind. But you don't want it to blow too hard. Too much wind can cause rough seas, which can be uncomfortable for sailors.

Wind is air that is moving. Blow hard against the inside of your hand: you will feel the movement in the air.

We can tell how hard the wind is blowing by using a special scale of 0 to 12 to measure wind force. When the wind is quiet, and nothing moves – not even leaves on a tree – the wind force is 0. If the wind blows so hard that trees fall over and tiles fly off rooftops, the wind force is 12. At wind force 5 or 6, there is already a storm, and most skippers are scratching their heads as they decide whether they should go out on the water or stay ashore.

Wind direction

When you go sailing, you not only want to know how hard the wind is blowing, but also which direction it's coming from. A wind is always named after the direction from which it blows. So, a south wind comes from the south and blows towards the north. Easy! You can see all the directions of the wind on a wind rose or a compass rose.

Do you want to know which way the wind is blowing? You can find out for yourself. Just look at a waving flag or the leaves on the trees. They move in the same direction the wind is blowing. Some boats have a small weathervane on board that shows where the wind is coming from. Or, wet your (clean!) index finger in your mouth and then hold it in the air. Where does it feel cold? That's where the wind is coming from!

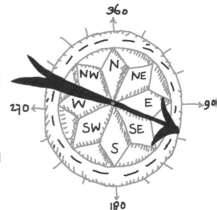

Wind in the sails

For the sailors among us, wind is essential for a boat trip. With the wind in the sails you can take to the open water! But to keep up the pace, you need to know not only where the wind is coming from, but also how the sails should be set. If you sail with the wind behind you, you will sail 'before the wind' and the wind will blow in the sails. The boat should be moving well! If you have a head wind, sailing will be a lot harder. The sail doesn't catch any wind and starts to flap. When you sail 'against the wind', as it's called, you don't move forwards. In fact, you're going backwards.

Luckily, there are other ways to keep up the pace. In the drawing below you can see exactly how it works. If the wind blows from a certain direction, you know which course you can take (and which you can't). You cannot sail in the dark area of the drawing.

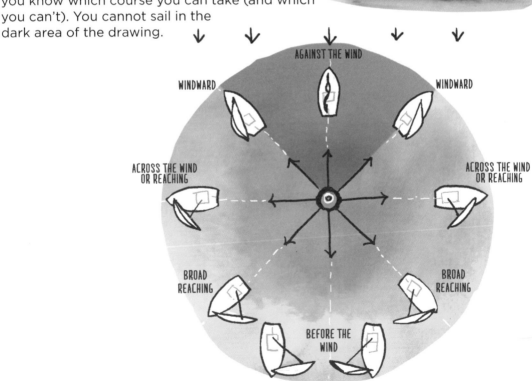

Playing with the wind

Experienced sailors can play with the wind and change the course of the sailboat. Of course, you can't change the wind itself, but you can change the position of the sails. Many sailors love the thrill of moving the sails from one side of the boat to the other to catch more wind.

This is called 'tacking' (when the wind comes from the front) or 'gybing' (if you have the wind in your back). But beware of gybes! The sail can suddenly swing to the other side due to strong winds. This is called a 'crash-gybe', and you have to mind your head or the sail may bash into you!

If the wind is favourable and blowing nicely in the sails, the sailor has little to do. That can be enjoyable sometimes. But you don't want to get too lazy, do you?

WIND ➡

ACTIVITY

1. Drawing clouds

I never get tired of clouds. I can watch them for hours. Try it! Lie down on your back in the grass – or on the deck – and look to the sky.

Think about what each cloud looks like. Can you see different shapes in the clouds? Take a photo of the most interesting shapes. Later, you can use your photos to draw what you saw. Of course, you can also draw clouds while you watch, but they can change shape quickly so you'll need to be fast!

I like to collect the funniest and craziest shapes. How about you?

2. Wind in the sails

Take a look at my drawings on the right. When do you have the wind in your sails? What course does the sailboat take?

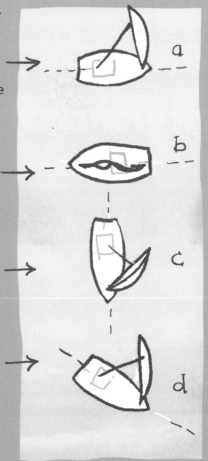

(a) Before the wind.
(b) Against the wind.
(c) Across the wind (reaching).
(d) Broadreaching.

3. Create a windvane

You can make your own windvane to help you know which direction the wind is coming from.

You will need:
- scissors
- thick cardboard
- two straws
- satay skewer (kebab stick)
- flowerpot and soil
- sheet of white paper
- felt tip pen
- ruler
- compass

Cut out a large triangle from a thick piece of cardboard. Cut off the tip of the triangle. You now have two pieces of cardboard.

Cut short lengthways slits in both ends of one straw, right in the middle. Push one side of the triangular piece of cardboard into the slit on one end of the straw. Repeat with the other piece of cardboard on the other end of the straw, as shown in the picture on the right.

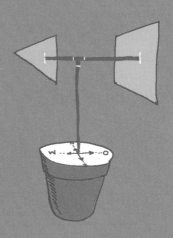

Use the skewer to pierce a hole in the middle of the straw that is holding the cardboard pieces.

Turn the flowerpot upside down on the paper and draw a circle around the rim. Cut it out. Using a ruler, draw a cross on the circle and add the wind directions N(orth), E(ast), S(outh) and W(est). Make a small hole in the middle of the circle.

Turn the flowerpot the right way up, fill it with soil, then place the paper circle on top. A compass will tell you which direction is north. Thread the skewer through the second straw, then stand it upright in the pot, through the hole in the paper circle. Slot the first straw on top, pushing the upright straw into the hole. Now, just let it swing.

CHAPTER 9

SPORT AND GAMES

DISCOVER & ACTIVITY

On a summer's day you can play and practise sports on and around the boat. Besides boating, what is your favourite hobby? Snorkelling underwater? Water sports or a game with water? Catching fish or crabs? Birdwatching? You don't ever have to be bored on a boat!

In the water

Snorkelling with a mask

There is much more happening than you think under the water. Go on a voyage of discovery! If you have a snorkel and a mask and flippers, and if you can swim well, you can snorkel in lots of places – from a river to a large lake – as long as you have a good view.

A lifejacket helps you stay afloat. Make sure it's safe to swim and an adult knows where you are.

Water polo with a dinghy

Do you like competing and can you tread water? Then I'm sure you'll love water polo! You'll need two teams, a ball and a goal – you can use an inflatable boat or a dinghy. Attach it to the big boat or a bollard on the shore. If you throw the ball in the boat, you score a point. The team with the most points at the end of the match wins!

Waddling in flippers

Have you ever tried to run while wearing flippers? It's hard, but funny: you'll waddle a bit like a penguin! For this game you'll need two large buckets (one filled with water) and a plastic cup. The aim is to carry the water from the full bucket to the empty bucket using the cup – while wearing flippers, of course! And don't spill any water along the way, OK? The winner is the first to fill the bucket and spill the least water.

Playing with the wind

As a sailor, you really need the wind. But while you're on shore, it's also fun to play with the wind. A beautiful kite flies playfully through the air! If you don't have a kite, you can attach a plastic bag to a long rope and use it to catch the wind. You'll be able to tell exactly which direction the wind is coming from. Make sure you take the plastic bag home with you when you've finished.

Making a shell necklace

It's fun to search for shells on the coast. You can start by looking for shells on beaches or in the mud at low tide.

Special shells are nice enough in themselves to deserve a place on the boat. But if you collect enough, you can make a shell necklace. First, you'll need to carefully make a hole in each shell using a mini drill. Make sure you ask the skipper to help you drill the holes. Line up the shells, then thread a string through the holes. If you put a button on the string between each shell, the shells will stay in place. All done!

Casting a fishing rod

When you are ashore, you can look for a spot to fish. There are plenty of places to choose from: you can cast your rod at the waterfront of a lake or canal, or from the jetty in a harbour. You can catch many species of fish. In the fresh waters inland, you may find roach and bream. They're the ones that get caught the most. Of course, as well as a fishing rod you need bait to catch fish. A piece of bread will do.

Watch out though! In many places, you'll need a fishing permit before you can fish, and some fish species are protected.

Catching crabs

Catching crabs is quite different to catching fish! You must be near the sea because crabs live in salt water. Did you know crabs love bacon?

You can make your own rod from a stick and a piece of rope. If you attach a stone at the bottom of the rope with a piece of bacon on top, the tasty bite for the crabs sinks to the bottom. That's where they are!

If your string moves, you have a bite. You can either put the crab in a bucket of sea water or back in the sea. Beware of its claws!

Water bugs in your catch

Even with a small fishing net you can have fun by the water. Chances are you'll catch water bugs in your net, as so many different types live in the water. You may have caught or seen a tadpole. Perhaps you'll catch a backswimmer or a water boatman? This small insect looks like an upturned boat, and it scoots across the surface of the water.

Making a campfire

It's fun to sit together around a campfire and sing songs! In some places, you are allowed to make a campfire. First, gather wooden branches, small and large. You'll need small twigs to start the fire. Remember to always find a safe spot and check with an adult, think about the wind direction and prepare a bucket of water, just in case.

If the fire burns well, you can toast marshmallows. Push a marshmallow on to the end of a long stick and hold it above (not in!) the heat. Turn the stick every now and then, until the marshmallow becomes nice and gooey. Yummy!

Birdwatching

There are always a lot of birds near water. If you're on a jetty in the harbour, it's likely that you'll see well-known waterfowl, such as ducks, herons and coots. But if you head out on the boat with binoculars to spot birds, with a little luck you will discover many more rare species! There is so much to learn about nature. Take a look at a bird guide to work out which bird is which.

Captain of your own ship

There's nothing quite like sailing in your very own boat. Whether it's an inflatable boat, a canoe or a rowing boat, you'll be the captain of your ship. Ahoy! You can also usually see a lot more below the surface from your own boat because you are low on the water. What is there to discover on the water and on the waterfront?

Sailing or surfing competitions

Are you sailing in your own Optimist or is there a surfboard on board? If the answer is yes then you can organise your own competition! Who can sail or surf the fastest?

AHOY!

ARE YOU A REAL SAILOR?

TAKE THE TEST!

Have you learned a lot about boating and boats? Did you take a good look around you while sailing? And as a sailor, did you help the skipper? I wonder if you're a real sailor now. Do you want to find out? Then take the test! If you manage to answer the questions correctly, I will award you with your own sailing diploma.

Are you ready? Here are nine questions. If you don't know the answers by heart, you can look them up.

1. What parts do only sailboats have? There's only one right answer. Which is it?
a. Hull, steering wheel, throttle, mast.
b. Mast, hull, cockpit, boom.
c. Engine, mast, rudder, hull.

2. Why can one boat sail faster than the other? Which answer is wrong?
a. It has a faster engine.
b. The shape of the boat glides more easily through the water.
c. The longer a boat is, the faster it sails.
d. You can always make a boat go faster by pressing on the gas.

3. What does 'good seamanship' mean?
a. You always greet other sailors on the water.
b. You learned to be a sailor and have a certificate.
c. You always do your best on the boat to avoid a collision.

4. How can you find your way on the water? Which answer is wrong?
a. By looking at which side of the water the red and green buoys and markers lie.
b. By studying the water map carefully.
c. By watching the wind.
d. By looking at the sun or the stars.

5. Why are there locks on canals and other inland waterways?
a.   Because it's fun to go up and down in the water.
b.   Because the water on inland waterways is not the same height everywhere:
     in a lock, the water gets higher and lower.
c.   Because the skippers on the boats in the lock can pay money to the lock
     keeper to be allowed to continue sailing.

6. What tasks do you have to complete as a sailor? Which answer is right?
a.   Scrubbing the deck, tying knots, helping to moor the boat.
b.   Scrubbing the deck, steering, tying knots.
c.   Tying knots, helping to moor the boat, steering.

**7. When a boat is built and is launched for the first time, there's usually a
     celebration. What happens then?**
a.   The flag is raised on the mast.
b.   The skipper and sailors sing sea shanties.
c.   A bottle of champagne is smashed against the boat.

**8. How do you know if it's going to be good or bad weather? Which answer
     is wrong?**
a.   You can watch the weather forecast on television.
b.   You can study the clouds.
c.   You can read the weather forecast on the internet.
d.   You can watch what direction the birds are flying in.

9. What does the phrase 'all hands on deck' mean?
a.   All crew members should wash their hands immediately.
b.   Everyone on board needs to help.
c.   All crew members should stop what they're doing and do a handstand.

You can check your answers on page 88.

If you have managed to answer all nine questions correctly, then
congratulations – you have earned your sailing diploma (see page 89)!
You can fill in your name and there's a space for the skipper to sign it.
Your sailing diploma deserves a nice spot on the boat!

Test answers

1. What parts do only sailboats have? There's only one right answer. Which is it?
b. Mast, hull, cockpit, boom.

2. Why can one boat sail faster than the other? Which answer is wrong?
d. You can always make a boat go faster by pressing on the gas.

3. What does 'good seamanship' mean?
c. You always do your best on the boat to avoid a collision.

4. How can you find your way on the water? Which answer is wrong?
c. By watching the wind.

5. Why are there locks on canals and other inland waterways?
b. Because the water on inland waterways is not the same height everywhere: in a lock, the water gets higher and lower.

6. What tasks do you have as a sailor? Which answer is the right one?
a. Scrubbing the deck, tying knots, helping to moor the boat.

7. When a boat has been built and it is launched for the first time, there's usually a celebration. What happens then?
c. A bottle of champagne is smashed against the boat.

8. How do you know if it's going to be good or bad weather? Which answer is wrong?
d. You can watch what direction the birds are flying in.

9. What does the phrase 'all hands on deck' mean?
b. Everyone on board needs to help.

Sailing Diploma

Sailor's name: ....

Skipper's signature:

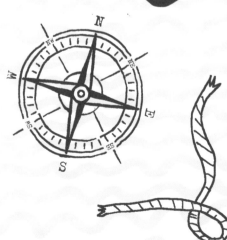

................

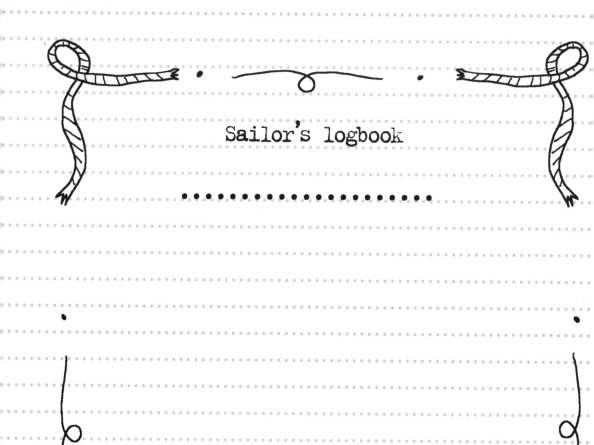

Sailor's logbook

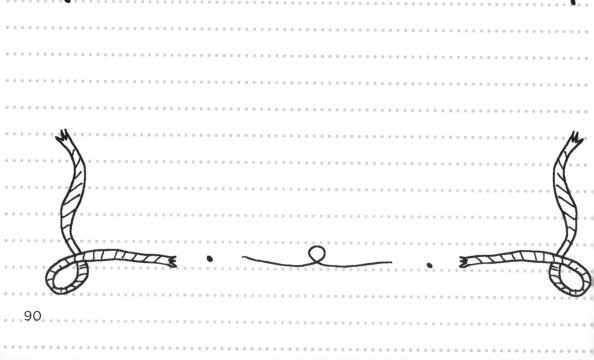

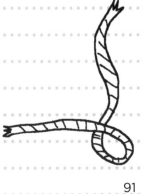

Your favourite recipe on board

Funny sayings

Draw your own flag

Word of thanks

As the author of this book, I have enjoyed working with:

Henk de Velde, who wrote the foreword and checked all the chapters for content.

Jan de Boer of the Marine Research Institute in Wageningen, who provided the content for Chapter 2, including the fun and instructive educational exercises for that chapter.

Charlotte Borggreve, author of several non-fiction children's books, who reviewed the first version of the chapters.

Casper Schaaf and **Silke Bouman** of the publishing house **Hollandia**.

And of course: **Ingrid Robers**, who drew **Sailor Taylor** and the other fantastic illustrations in this book.

Lisette Vos

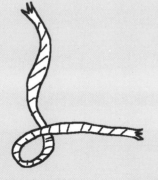